STAR BIOGRAPHIES

CAMILA CABELLO

Fly!
An Imprint of Abdo Zoom
abdobooks.com

ENNY ABDO

abdobooks.com

Published by Abdo Zoom, a division of ABDO, P.O. Box 398166, Minneapolis, Minnesota 55439. Copyright © 2019 by Abdo Consulting Group, Inc. International copyrights reserved in all countries. No part of this book may be reproduced in any form without written permission from the publisher. Fly!™ is a trademark and logo of Abdo Zoom.

Printed in the United States of America, North Mankato, Minnesota.
092018
012019

 THIS BOOK CONTAINS RECYCLED MATERIALS

Photo Credits: Alamy, AP Images, Everette Collection, flickr, Getty Images, iStock, Shutterstock, ©Jordan Strauss/Invision/AP/Shutterstock p11
Production Contributors: Kenny Abdo, Jennie Forsberg, Grace Hansen
Design Contributors: Dorothy Toth, Neil Klinepier

Library of Congress Control Number: 2018946320

Publisher's Cataloging-in-Publication Data

Names: Abdo, Kenny, author.
Title: Camila Cabello / by Kenny Abdo.
Description: Minneapolis, Minnesota : Abdo Zoom, 2019 | Series: Star biographies
      | Includes online resources and index.
Identifiers: ISBN 9781532125423 (lib. bdg.) | ISBN 9781641856874 (pbk) |
      ISBN 9781532126444 (ebook) | ISBN 9781532126956 (Read-to-me ebook)
Subjects: LCSH: Cabello, Camila, 1997- (Karla Camila Cabello Estrabao)--
      Juvenile literature. | Singers--Biography--Juvenile literature. | Popular music--
      Juvenile literature. | Musicians--Biography--Juvenile literature.
Classification: DDC 782.4216409 [B]--dc23

TABLE OF CONTENTS

CAMILA CABELLO

Camila Cabello is a rising
star who lights up music
charts and TVs around the
world. She made a name
for herself in the pop super
group Fifth Harmony. Today,
she is a solo artist.

EARLY YEARS

Karla Camila Cabello Estrabao was born in Cojimar, Cuba, in 1997.

Florida

■ MIAMI

The Bahamas

COJIMAR

Cuba

Haiti

Dominican Republic

Jamaica

Her family moved from Havana to Mexico City, Mexico, when she was a baby. They finally landed in Miami, Florida, when she was five years old.

Camila left high school during her **freshman** year. She wanted to pursue her dream of becoming a famous singer.

THE BIG TIME

Cabello **auditioned** for *The X Factor* when she was 15 years old. She was cut early on in the competition.

Soon, Cabello was brought back on the show to form the all-girl group Fifth Harmony. She was joined by Normani, Lauren Jauregui, Dinah Jane, and Ally Brooke.

Fifth Harmony finished in third place. They signed a **record deal** shortly after. They made two albums together.

Cabello left Fifth Harmony in 2016. She released her first solo album, *Camila,* in 2018. She has also dropped five **singles**.

Her **single**, *Havana*, topped the *Billboard* pop **chart**. Cabello was #1 longer than any other female solo artist in the last five years!

LEGACY

Cabello is the first artist to top the Pop Songs and Adult Pop Songs radio airplay **charts** with the first two **singles** from her **debut** album.

VIRGINIA BLACK

She won the Artist of the Year award at the 2018 *MTV Video Music Awards*. Cabello also won Music Video of the Year award for her song *Havana*.

GLOSSARY

audition – a trial performance showcasing personal talent as a musician, singer, dancer, or actor.

chart – a list that shows which music has sold the most during a period of time.

debut – a first appearance.

freshman – a first-year student.

record deal – a legally written agreement to perform for one record label.

single – a song released to promote a whole album.

ONLINE RESOURCES

Booklinks
NONFICTION NETWORK
FREE! ONLINE NONFICTION RESOURCES

To learn more about Camila Cabello, please visit **abdobooklinks.com**. These links are routinely monitored and updated to provide the most current information available.

INDEX